HERE TODAY
by Alan Wright

JOHN LENNON
IN THE 21ST CENTURY

This edition first published in paperback by
Michael Terence Publishing in 2022
www.mtp.agency

Copyright © 2022 Alan Wright

Alan Wright has asserted the right to be identified as
the author of this work in accordance with the
Copyright, Designs and Patents Act 1988

ISBN 9781800944473

No part of this publication may be reproduced, stored
in a retrieval system, or transmitted, in any form or
by any means, electronic, mechanical, photocopying,
recording or otherwise, without the prior
permission of the publisher

Cover image
by courtesy of Alan Wright

Cover design
Copyright © 2022 Michael Terence Publishing

Contents

1: The Concert for George 1
2: I Ching 4
3: Thrown Together 7
4: Summer 1980 10
5: Later That Summer 13
6: Autumn 1980 15
7: December 9th, 1980 17
8: January 1981 20
9: Having a Lovely Time 27
10: Bitte Schon Hamburg 31
11: Pay It Again Sam 38
12: Ringoing The Changes 41
13: While My Guitar… 48
14: When I Was Younger, So Much Younger Than Today . 55
15: Starting Over 62
16: Shall I Compare Thee To The Twilight Zone? 68
17: Back To Bed? 73
18: Here There and Everywhere 82
19: New York City 87
20: Tomorrow Never Knows 91

1

The Concert for George

Sunday, December 8th, 2002
BBC Television Centre, London, England
The Michael Parkinson Show, Live

Good evening and thank you for joining me.

I've seen hundreds of shows over the years, but never something like last week when I was privileged to be in the audience for A Concert for George.

A year to the day after we lost George Harrison, many of his friends came together to celebrate a famous life and talent. The evening brought smiles and tears and it was simply remarkable.

One of the big names sharing his music was his long-time friend and a fellow Beatle and he's with us this evening. Will you please welcome – John Lennon.

Good to be here Mike. It's over thirty years since I was on your show, so it's good to have a regular gig!

You were nervous about having me and Yoko on as guests back in 1971 weren't you? You only gave us half the show with another guest on for the second half in case we did something daft.

Spot on, but you were great and very funny. It felt awful to have to cut you short, but you are a changed man now. I could see that in the Concert for George; you look at peace with yourself.

Just being in the audience hit me hard John, so how did it feel for you being on stage in the middle of it all?

Unbelievable. Do you remember what Ravi Shankar said at the start of the evening? He said that George must be with us; how can he not be when so many people that loved him are here tonight.

It wasn't just words you know. When I was a kid in Liverpool, I used to laugh at the idea of being spiritual, but not anymore.

But the main thing I felt all night was guilty.

Why guilty?

Well, George was the youngest of the four of us and, as Paul always says, like our little brother. So, I should have gone first. Should have been me.

Must be the journalist in me John, but I keep checking dates and co-incidences. It's probably in your head too, but twenty two years ago today, it could have been you. If you had still been living in New York, it would have been you that Chapman murdered.

Hell, I know it, and it's another reason for feeling guilty that an innocent guy died instead of me.

And it's not a co-incidence by the way. There's no such thing.

It was George who taught me that. We all tried, but he was the leader in getting to the heart of life.

He turned me on to the Chinese philosophy book I Ching, the Book of Changes. I get it now. It says that everything is relative to everything else, not like the Western view that things are merely co-incidental. He told me that he wrote one of his best ever songs that way. He opened a book and the first two words he saw were "gently weeps". Of course, you need to be a genius of a composer to go the next step and turn that into While my Guitar Gently Weeps.

And was he a genius?

He was. I think he felt himself in the shadow of Paul and myself but he was up there with us. I wish we'd have told him more often.

And those two angles of being spiritual and everything being relative. Is that why you weren't in New York City in December 1980?

Exactly Michael. You are really bright for a Yorkshireman.

Thank you.

It's ok, I didn't mean it.

And you have always been a superb diplomat – didn't mean that either.

(Laughing). We'll get on well Mike.

2
I Ching

April 23rd, 1980
Dakota Building, New York City
The Lennons' Apartment

I'm honestly trying to understand what you are telling me Yoko, but I'm struggling.

Don't worry John; we have all the time in the world. Your difficulty comes because my culture is based in the East and yours is in the West.

That Chinese book you gave me – the I Ching – I've been trying to read it but it fogs my head after a while.

Take it slowly, and remember that, for now, you just need to give in and accept a few of its basic ideas.

Your life is perfect proof of its key philosophy; there are no coincidences in life. What brought you and the other guys together to produce the Beatles wasn't just chance. It was all planned out before you were born.

Don't forget that I Ching, the Book of Changes, has been around for over three thousand years and it's been well and truly tested.

Scholars and philosophers have taken it apart and the line I like is the one associating knowledge of the I Ching with the ability to delight in Heaven and understand fate.

Once you get that you will see patterns emerging and not despair when you meet a few bumps along the way.

Focus for now on what it means for you and for us.

Even though the whole I Ching concept is ancient, it's still modern. If you really want your brain fogged, read up about how it predates linear algebra and logic in computer science by centuries. And then you can move on to quantum mechanics and how Yin and Yang symbolism inspired it all.

Don't!

Oh, all that's for later if it all. I do know that you were searching for the I Ching answers long before I met you.

You mean India and the Maharishi?

Exactly. You guys had seen some of the world, you'd made more money than you'd ever seen before, and now you wanted to know what else was in life and beyond.

That's so true. A lot of the trip was disappointing but George was miles ahead of us in seeing a bigger picture.

He really worked out what was important long before the rest of us.

I remember him saying once,

"Like, we're the Beatles after all, aren't we. We have all the money you could ever dream of. We have all the fame you could ever wish for. But it isn't love. It isn't health. It isn't peace inside. Is it?"

He told me about the whole I Ching thing but I was too full of myself to get it.

He was even inspired from that to take a couple of apparently random words and see where they led. I still can't believe he did that. Flicked open a book, saw "gently weeps", and came up with While My Guitar Gently Weeps. It was better than just about anything Paul and I ever wrote. I wish I'd told him when he was still alive.

This is great John; you are opening your mind to I Ching, and that's the start of the path.

And while you are feeling receptive can I tell you about some advice from my astrologer?

I'll give it a go – your astrologer sounds sensible compared to the newspaper versions that the four of us always used to laugh about.

I know some people took them seriously, but they were hilarious. Your so-called horoscope would tell you in June that you may be going on a trip soon, and the one for early December told you that you might be due to receive a gift!

And of course, the Zodiac was split into twelve groups so each slot would fit about five million people. Always a fighting chance that a prediction might fit.

I agree John and I've told you before that rubbish like that gives meaningful advice a bad name.

My astrologer's advice for you was very specific – you need to make a trip by sea to the south east. Looks like Bermuda.

3
Thrown Together

So why does it need to be a sea journey? I could fly it in a couple of hours.

True John, but my astrologer says that going by sea under sail will test you and develop your mind.

I think I'd enjoy it, but I'd need a hand. Those sailing lessons I've been taking have been in the little boat around the size of a bath tub – and I've done a few miles in total. Six hundred miles or so to Bermuda would be something else.

Of course. Like most things in life, you'll need a little help from your friends; your sailing teacher friend could look after you and get you there safely.

I'll do it then. What could go wrong?

A lot will go right. Remember – delight in Heaven and understand fate.

My astrologer is way ahead of me in wisdom and insight – he sees something in this sea trip of yours that we don't know about yet. Even if something did go wrong, there would be a reason and something good for you to come from it.

Every time I've sat and listened to you about your life, I've picked out patterns which you have never seen because you are too close to it all.

Which patterns? I've had an ordinary life except for being lucky a few times.

Ordinary? So, when you were a kid in Liverpool you could picture sitting here with me in New York as one of the biggest names in the world?

You are right – of course not, but what are these patterns you are talking about?

There are so many that I've started keeping notes. Let's start with the biggest one – why did you and Paul come together and why do you get on so well – most of the time?

We just clicked and it was like we were thrown together.

You are nearly there – but what threw you together? You both had tough breaks early on, but, without them, you wouldn't have had such a good personality fit.

Most men have a mother well into later life but look what happened to you two. Paul lost his mother when he was only fourteen and you lost yours when you were seventeen. That's a strong connection for a start.

I know it still hurts for you to talk about your mother and it sounds like Julia was an amazing woman.

She really was and I miss her every day. That night she died was horrible. She'd just fixed for me to go and live with her sister Mimi, mainly to save some cash at home. Then – wrong place and wrong time – she's hit by a car and was killed instantly.

I felt really lonely after that, even with people around me. I know I became mentally harder and developed a weird sense of humour.

This might sound cruel John, but perhaps living with Mimi was part of Heaven's plan. She was a special woman too, and how many women did you know then who could play banjo and teach you those odd chords?

I know how much Julia still means to you. Do you remember last year when you started recording your life story on that little cassette machine?

You whizzed through a lot of things but really lingered over her. And your Julia song is something else. Any woman would be proud to have a love song like that written about her.

And I was listening just the other day to your In My Life song that you recorded ages ago.

There are places I remember
All my life, though some have changed
Some forever not for better
Some have gone and some remain

I was musing that perhaps Julia was in that song too.

Perhaps you know me better than I know myself.

Oh, I've known that for a while.

4
Summer 1980

You know Yoko, I've never felt so pleased to be sitting in a comfortable chair with a phone in my hand.

Your astrologer was right about that journey testing me. The weather forecaster wasn't as good as your guy; the calm forecast turned into one hell of a storm.

I was terrified John. There was no way of making contact and I thought I'd lost you. Thank Heaven you are safe.

It feels like a bad dream now, but whatever happened at sea recharged me.

That boat felt tiny once the clear skies disappeared after Rhode Island and the storm began. Our skipper reckoned that the winds were hitting 120 miles per hour and the biggest waves were over 20 feet high.

I was supposed to be in charge of the cooking and my little galley was doing fine. Then Captain Hank was awake for three days straight trying to keep us on course and the other guys were rough and seasick.

He looked me straight in the eye and told me that I was now in charge of steering just before he went below to sleep.

So, I was there driving the boat for six hours, keeping it on course. I remembered the little I'd learned and it worked.

I was buried under water. I was smashed in the face by waves for six solid hours. It won't go away. You can't change your mind. It's like being on stage. Once you're on there's no gettin' off.

A couple of the waves had me on my knees. I was just hanging on with my hands on the wheel – it's very powerful weather – and I was having the time of my life. I was screaming sea shanties and shoutin' at the gods!

I think Hank was expecting to die in his sleep but he was staggered that I'd made it into calmer weather.

How about me? An ordinary kid from Liverpool who can now sail a boat through a massive storm.

Once we sailed into the harbour in St George's I felt so much at home.

We went for a walk and it's just like England. Nice people, and they even drive on the left. I love New York like you, but it's been years since I've been home and I didn't realise how much I'd missed it.

The guys took me for a celebration drink on Front Street in Hamilton last night and the music was something else. I was listening to Rock Lobster by the B52s and it blew my head off.

I haven't finished writing a song in five years, but I'm back on the case now – and how.

I've found a house to rent and it's just right. The district has a great name – Fairylands – and I hope you'll come to see it soon. It's nothing like the Dakota or New York City, but you'll love it. It's so peaceful and welcoming.

5
Later That Summer

Yoko, I'm beyond happy that you are here in Bermuda with me. We can find the perfect family home for us and we're only a couple of hours from New York so we can visit whenever we like.

I know why you love the city and I feel the same. When I first went there, it was like the place I wanted to be all my life. I suppose from being a kid, the States and New York were all glamour with the music and the look of life. Every film and TV show I saw tempted me more.

Everything is happening there and every day and night there's something fascinating right next to the Dakota.

You have me well sold on Bermuda John; I'm in love with the place. As you say we have the luxury of a private plane any time we like and we can be back in New York in not much more than an hour.

I'm glad that we flew Sean down afterwards, he'd have gone off travel for life if he was on your sailboat!

And I'm so grateful that your wisdom, and I Ching, taught me the meaning of success.

And your astrologer guy had it just right – the good and bad of that journey really worked.

I was so centred after that sea journey that I was tuned in, or whatever, to the cosmos. And the songs won't stop coming. It's just amazing. It reminds me of the early days with Paul when we had this torrent of tunes coming out. Except now I'm sitting on the beach with a guitar instead of being in a bedroom in a small house in Liverpool.

6
Autumn 1980

Well Mrs Lennon, we Brits have traditions too, so I take great pride in carrying you over the threshold of our forever home in Hamilton.

I love this place John. After a lot of looking, this place really clicked. Our own little island and the garden for Sean. Even a little dock for our sailboat for my expert sailor husband.

And the builders and techie guys are great. Our own studio will be finished soon. A two minute walk across our garden to a state of the art set-up. I'll have friends from everywhere in the world wanting to record here.

Can you imagine such great days. Enjoying making music again then chilling out with friends while we watch the sun go down over the sea.

I've just phoned the Hit Factory studios in New York to cancel our booking because we have our own facility now. They were great and said we are always welcome there if we have some other work to do.

It feels so safe here and, just like New York to be fair, nobody bothers me much.

It's great just wandering and Sean's having a great time too. We love those old streets in St George's and he keeps making up stories about the people who lived there. I wonder who he gets that from. He's only four, but has one hell of a creative mind, courtesy of both of us.

We both love the Botanical Gardens in Hamilton. It's a kind of therapy and meditation to stop and stare at a flower; just to take in its scent and sheer beauty. I can even name them now. I found a flower called Double Fantasy and I thought it would be a great name for our new album. It says a lot in two words you know.

As soon as the studio is all done we can get in there together with a band and really work.

7
December 9th, 1980

Well Mrs Lennon, we look like a very content couple. Morning coffee and the newspapers, a view of the sea, and ready to get back into our studio. It feels great.

It really does. And there's a picture of the Dakota Building here in the paper.

Oh, hell no!

What happened?

Put your coffee down and listen to this.

"A man was killed in a shooting outside the Dakota Building in New York City yesterday. The building achieved new fame as the former home of the musician John Lennon and his wife Yoko and early reports suggest that the murder victim had a strange link.

Friends of the victim have supplied unconfirmed reports that the man was Robert Brown who worked as a John Lennon lookalike in a Beatles tribute band. He had gone to the Dakota for a photoshoot as part of a publicity campaign.

He had visited the Dakota earlier in the day to meet the photographer who had been held up on another assignment. The victim apparently looks so much like Lennon that he signed autographs. Later in the day he returned and lost his life.

We will have more detail soon. Our thoughts are with the victim's family and friends."

Two Days Later

You are still looking numb John and I'm not surprised but please remember that the poor guy at the Dakota was not your fault. It's Heaven and fate again – he was in the wrong place and you were in the right place.

You've done all you can – getting in touch with his family was the right thing to do even though you didn't need to. And you've kept it private and offered all the support they'll want. You are a good man John.

Just think, though. Without the sailing trip advice, it would have been you outside the Dakota a few days ago.

Without all that, I wouldn't be getting close to Paul again.

We've had our ups and downs, but I'm still so pleased that he was the first person to ring after the news broke.

We had another two hours on the phone this morning and he's really warming to the I Ching philosophy. He really wants to talk it through when he comes to visit soon. He'll arrive first and Linda is going to spend a few days with her family in the States before she follows him.

8
January 1981

I can see why you love it here John. What a great country and such a top place to be – and your studio! Wow! It's like Abbey Road but years ahead.

You are too kind Paul. See, I'm sounding like an English gentleman now instead of a nobody from Liverpool. I want you to listen to what we've been recording in the studio – it will be great to have your opinion. I value it more than you'll know.

You've never been a nobody John and I'm really wanting to hear what you've done – and to make music together again. Despite all the odd disagreements along the way, we have a bond that's special. As you say, "it's only us." It often works best when it is only us – I guess we have to have them, but the lawyers and the money guys seem to make life harder than it need be.

I've been thinking about this whole Heaven and fate thing from Yoko and I really get it. I feel really sad for the poor guy who died at the Dakota building, but without you taking that sea trip and living in Bermuda now, I'd have lost my best friend.

And Yoko is so sharp. She picked up straight away the link we had because we both lost our mothers when we were young, and lots of other things too.

I'd love to talk through all those weird things in our lives early on, but I can I tell you about a few things between the two of us?

Of course, you know that.

Well, I share everything with Linda, mostly, but this is about Jane Asher, before I met Linda, and it might unsettle her.

It still unsettles me too Paul. She was gorgeous and do you remember that we all thought she was blonde? We'd only seen her pictures in black and white and it was a shock when she turned up with that flaming red hair.

We all tried to pull her but you won. Hell, when was that?

1963 – nearly forty years ago!

The more I thought about that, the more it fitted with the I Ching philosophy and things happening for a reason.

For a start, she'd been sent to see us at the Royal Albert Hall by Radio Times magazine. That was a big outfit in those days and they could have sent any of their writers. But it was her.

And it wasn't just about us becoming a couple – it had an even bigger impact because of her family.

Do you remember how it all felt then John. It was like waking up in a new world after being kids in Liverpool and staying in really crap rooms when we were learning the trade in Hamburg.

Brian Epstein impressed us when he found us our apartment in Mayfair, about as posh as we'd ever seen. I can't remember why but I was the last one to go and take a look at it. By then, you three had bagged the best rooms and I was left with this tiny rabbit hutch.

I was lucky to have another option because of Jane and her family. Not just the room they gave me, but they were like nothing I knew from Liverpool days.

She was classy as hell and her parents were something else. Her father Richard was a top doctor and her mother Margaret was a music teacher. She had the grandest title I'd ever heard – Professor of Oboe at the Guildhall School of Music and Drama. Would you believe that one of her pupils had been George Martin? He studied piano and oboe there in the late Forties – and look at all he's done for us.

It was more than that though. She was like having a mother again – she was special. I'd only seen working class Liverpool really but she and her family opened windows on a new world for me.

And talk about welcoming. The size of their house meant that they had space to spare and she more or less decided – "You are here to see Jane so often, you might as well have the room in the attic."

So that's what I did, and they even put a piano up there for me.

Do you remember when you came to visit John and we used the basement room with another piano where Margaret used to teach her students? We'd write there, both on the piano at the same time, or eyeball to eyeball on our guitars.

Jane's parents seemed to know everybody in London and I was soon spending time at concerts or museums and reading writers who were all knew to me.

And just think – if the Radio Times had sent somebody ordinary to interview us, none of that would have happened.

Alan Wright

It was totally my fault that Jane and I broke up. I even wrote We Can Work It Out for her. But we couldn't.

When I broke up with Jane, I lost Margaret too. It was like losing my mum for the second time.

I'll never forget what Jane and her family did for me, and I love them for it.

I think we are becoming better men with women Paul. It wasn't just about the wild times in Hamburg or on tour, it was almost like the working class bloke's attitude to women at work.

A miner would never dream of taking a woman down the pit and most men believed that their working world was a closed space with no room for a female.

We kind of built a screen around us that nobody else could penetrate. That's why we had code words and in jokes to keep other people out.

It's probably why I messed it up with Cynthia and I'm working my socks off to get it right with Yoko.

Anyway, we need to talk further – and it will show how we

have changed to have Yoko and Linda involved.

And let's get back to working on music together again. It's always worked so well for us. For we two, it's not one and one making two; it's one and one making ten.

Dead right! That We Can Work It Out started as an ok song and ended up really well when you and George helped a lot.

It kicked off as Try to See It my Way because that's what I was trying to tell Jane when we weren't hitting it off. The words came when I felt bad after an argument and, you know how it is, you can't write that kind of song two weeks later. You just have to do it immediately. You can say things in a song that you might not say to the other person.

I remember getting the first couple of verses done then you coming up with the middle eight at your house. When we took it into the studio, George suggested that waltz pattern and those suspended triplets. I really remember listening to the whole process with a kind of awe, hearing that sense of friction and fracture.

I'm even looking back on it differently with the I Ching pattern in my head. It's just like it wasn't just us working on that track; there was some Heaven and fate involved as well.

Alan Wright

When you are ready Paul, have a listen to the tracks that Yoko and I recorded here before Christmas. It's all set to go in the studio listed under Double Fantasy. That's another bit of non-coincidence. Sean and I were walking in the botanical gardens here and they are amazing. We saw this beautiful freesia called Double Fantasy and it just felt right as a great album title.

Have a listen by yourself and then tell me what you think – I really care about what you have to say.

9
Having a Lovely Time

You're looking wide awake Paul. I'll need a few coffees to catch up.

Would you believe that I've been up since about four; my head was spinning with memories after our nostalgia fest yesterday and I wanted to hear your album as soon as I could. I cranked it up – hope I didn't disturb you.

Didn't hear a thing. Building that studio in the garden with NASA level soundproofing was one of my better ideas.

I loved so much of it.

Your song Woman is great. It caught a lot of what I've been thinking. You know what we were saying yesterday about shutting women out of our world in days gone by?

We are thinking about being with women now instead of just using them. Writing Girl or She Was Just Seventeen. Great songs still, but that was us then and Woman is us now.
And I loved the end of one track where you just about

breathed "In Bermuda, having a lovely time."

I really am Paul and it's great to feel music bursting out of me like the old days. Whatever happened in that storm was good for me. I'd written just about nothing for five years before that and I have more than twenty five new songs since I came here.

I wrote down a couple of lines I really loved; I wish I'd have thought of them.

Woman, I know you understand the little child inside the man.

Pass me that guitar John.

There you go, I've nearly learned it!

I was always impressed at how you could pick up a standard right handed guitar and play it upside down with your left hand!

I had to – always guitars around but none for left handers unless I brought my own.

Consider it done – next time you are here there'll be a

couple of left handers among this lot.

I was trying to remember what your "little child" reminded me of and then it clicked.

I know you liked people to think of you as the tough guy but I can recall your voice when you wrote that lullaby for young Julian when he was only five or so.

You called it "Goodnight" and I can't recall if you ever recorded it, but I can hear your voice now when you were singing it for Ringo to record.

At that time, you would have hated for anybody to call you tender and loving, but that's just how you were – and are.

You are making me blush now, but you're right, that's how I was underneath. I can see George Martin looking as surprised as hell when I asked him to give it a really lush orchestral arrangement just like the old Hollywood films.

And how about hard as nails Ringo whispering at the end of his recording.

"Good night. Good night everybody. Everybody everywhere. Goodnight."

Alan Wright

Look at the two of us – filling up like two old fogies.

10

Bitte Schon Hamburg

This I Ching stuff John; do you think that's what sent us to play in Hamburg?

I think it was you know. We went through some hard times but we learned a lot with playing those stupid long stints didn't we?

Just as well we can think back to those days without our ladies around. Hell, we were wild.

They are wise enough to know that we weren't living in a monastery, but best to keep it between us.

I was thinking the other day about the trip out there. We get spoiled with first class travel and private planes these days, but do you remember that van? It could have been a death trap.

None of us had been out of the country before and we were kind of excited – and innocent.

I can still picture George climbing into the van – he was only seventeen and holding a tin of scones his mother had baked for him.

Yep, just seventeen, you know what I mean?

Nice one!

My dad tried to talk me out of it but he gave in. The contract was for about seventeen quid a week- more than he was making, so he saw the point in the end.

Allan being our kind of manager thought we were heading for the big time with that Austin van.

Were there eight of us crammed in there with luggage and stuff?

Worse than that I think. Up front Allan was driving along with his wife Beryl and her brother Barry. Then Allan's business partner – can't remember his real name but we all called him Lord Woodbine cos he chain smoked them.

And how could we forget George Sterner? He was the right hand man for Bruno Koschmider and he had his club contract for us in his pocket.

And that bloody trek! These days you can fly from England to Hamburg in an hour or so, but that van took over a day.

Do you remember hanging about for about six hours in Newhaven, then the big argument on the other side at Hook of Holland?

They told Allan that we needed work permits and visas, but he conned them into believing that we were students so didn't need them.

After all that trek crammed in that noisy van, our eyes were just about closing, but then we rolled into the Reeperbahn in Hamburg and couldn't believe it.

I remember thinking that we won the war and they didn't but the place was bouncing. We'd never seen so many neon lights before – or naked women in shop windows!

And the streets were packed – obviously a lot of people had

money in their pockets.

That "what if" angle from I Ching worked for Hamburg as well.

I didn't find out until ages later that we weren't even Allan's first choice to go to Hamburg.

I knew he'd sent Derry and the Seniors out there and they were doing well and he was looking to send another British group.

The funniest thing is that it turned out that he'd tried to book Rory Storm and the Hurricanes but they were already booked at a Butlin's holiday camp so they turned him down. Ringo told me all about that cos he was their drummer before he was ours.

He asked Gerry Marsden with the Pacemakers as well but they were busy.

In the end, he sent us to the Indra in Hamburg until he found somebody better. Bloody charming that!

And he told us to find a drummer fast. You didn't have many drummers around cos a drum kit cost a lot more than a guitar. We persuaded Pete Best to join us with promises of big money and luxury accommodation in Hamburg. Yeah, right! He was all set to go to teacher training college and came with us instead.

It's funny now, but what about Bruno's "luxury accommodation" for us. We didn't dare tell anybody back home just how bad it was. Two dark and grubby rooms and the smell from the club's toilet coming through the thin wall – as well as the sounds of toilet activity. Sure, wasn't the Ritz.

Then again – I Ching again – at least we were somewhere and about to learn how to play in front of an audience.

The months before we went out there were dead. We'd failed to get through to a television talent show, failed to become Billy Fury's backing band, and failed to make much money.

Our first show at the Indra didn't impress Bruno much.

"You boys are crap. I wanted you to bring some fire and energy. All the German pop groups look dull and half asleep, but you make them look good."

I can hear him now screaming at us "Mach Schau boys." And we sure did start making a show.

Pete was sitting behind his drums looking well fed up and amazed at us being crazy in front of him. Then again he was the only one of us who wasn't taking stimulants like sweets.

We had such a lousy lifestyle it's amazing we survived.

Do you remember Harold's Café? Wasn't it just around the corner in Grosse Freiheit?

That's the one. We lived on egg and chips – and cornflakes and milk.

And do you remember the hamburgers? Except they called them frikadelle, those little meatballs. Could never understand why they didn't call them hamburgers in bloody Hamburg!

You were a bit off the wall then Paul. We all fancied Astrid Kircherr but she was Stu's girlfriend and it wasn't a bright move to say something saucy about her on stage. After he punched you and the fight began it actually improved our reputation with the punters.

Those Preludin tablets were supposed to be on prescription but Stu had a supply line through Astrid's mother. They kept you wideawake and hyper active and you took more than anybody John – and it showed a bit.

I suppose even Bruno thought we were taking making show a bit over the top. Fighting on stage, throwing food at the audience along with Nazi insults and salutes. Yeah, it was a bit strong.

The best night was when the boss caught me in the toilet with a lady when I should have been on stage.

He said, "you act like dogs so I treat you like dogs" and threw a bucket of water over us. He told the girl to get out of his club and ordered me to get back on stage.

So, I did – dripping wet, toilet seat around my neck, only underpants on and chanting Sieg Heil.

Bruno was in the audience so I shouted, "How's that for making show you kraut bastard?"

And the audience cheered me. They love suave scouse badinage that lot.

In the end, all those long hours on stage did improve us as a band. As long as were being loud, the crowd were fine. One of their favourites was What'd I Say and we broke our own record by playing it for ninety minutes non-stop one night. We did a lot of long tunes like that and loads of proper guitar.

We learned harmonies and good solos and soon the other bands were coming to see us instead of the other way round.

Allan came over and was amazed. We'd gone from a stop gap act to, in his words, "nobody in Liverpool could touch us."

It went downhill soon after though didn't it?

Our fault I guess. Breaking our contract to earn more money at the Top Ten Club annoyed Bruno a bit with it being a Hamburg competitor. He was bloody inventive in getting us out at high speed.

George deported for being too young to work, you and Pete for arson in his club.

That was special. We made a little mark on his concrete wall cos we couldn't see in the dark. If we'd have burned down the whole shambolic wreck, it would have been a tenner's worth of damage.

And then he got my work permit cancelled so we were all royally stuffed.

It was only Stu who stayed behind; engaged to Astrid and keener to be an art student than a Beatle.

I always felt guilty about us persuading Stu to spend a big chunk of his money on something he didn't really want.

The other Liverpool groups were looking better than us because they had better instruments and we'd tried to persuade people to buy a bass and join us but had no luck.

I kept saying that playing a bass couldn't be that hard – it only had four bloody strings.

Way back in 1959 Stu had some of his paintings in an art exhibition in Liverpool. It was sponsored by a local millionaire called John Moores, and, on the very last day they were on show, the guy himself bought one of Stu's paintings for £65. That was a lot of money then and he was looking forward to spending it on good quality art supplies.

We'd seen a beautiful Hofner bass guitar in a local music shop and we nagged him and just about frogmarched him round to buy it.

It looked beautiful and made us look more like a proper group. It was bigger than him and he couldn't play it, but there you go.

I did owe a lot to that guy. He knew about really clever stuff like philosophy and existentialism and I learned enough from him to con people into thinking I knew a bit as well.

11
Pay It Again Sam

Once we got home that December – 1960 it must have been – it felt like we just needed to hide.

All our big talk about heading off to be international stars and there we were back in Liverpool with no money, no prospects, and even our gear stuck in Hamburg.

And we'd even lost Stu when he decided to stay there with Astrid and be an artist.

And everyone else at home seemed to have moved on – the Swinging Blue Jeans were top dogs and all of the groups looked like the Shadows with sharp suits.

To be fair, Mimi tried to humour me even though she felt as if the music game was all over for us.

I felt really depressed after those highs in Hamburg and I feel bad for refusing to talk to anyone.

George didn't even know we were back for a while.

My dad was a bit heavy on me. He told me to get a proper job and do some music on the side. I got that job at Massey & Coggins and was doing ok; seven quid a week and ready for promotion!

I was all set to forget the music until you and George turned up at the factory telling me about the lunchtime booking at the Cavern.

Here Today – John Lennon in the 21st Century

I remember you bunked off work twice to play with us for the Cavern gigs, but then the factory told you that if it happened again you were fired.

I nearly stayed at the factory because my dad would have hit the roof if I'd have jacked in a steady job.

Hell, I remember hitting the roof as well, and shouting at you on the phone that if you didn't turn up for the next gig that you were out of the band and we'd find somebody else.

I guess I jumped the right way and became a Beatle. The week after that though I had my last wage packet from Massey and Coggins and felt real panic that I'd thrown my future away. My dad was sure that I'd done just that and told me ten times a day.

It started to work didn't it? All that time slogging away in Hamburg showed on stage and we were ready to move up the ladder.

And that I Ching philosophy has its losers too I take it. Do you remember Sam Leach and bloody Aldershot?

It's engraved on my heart! I loved Sam and he did really well at first fixing us bookings around Liverpool and beyond but then he made one big mistake, or perhaps two.

If he had got things right, he could have been a millionaire like Brian Epstein but he got it wrong.

Sam was a lovely guy but not the sharpest tool in the box as a businessman.

He was right in thinking that we needed to be seen and become big in London, but why the hell did he choose Aldershot? It's outside London, hardly the West End, and was more likely to have squaddies fighting in the street than top agents who could have done us some good.

Sam said himself that the wasn't good on details or paperwork and he wasn't kidding.

He'd fixed a poster and booked an ad in the local paper which would have filled the place, but, typical Sam, he didn't read the contract.

It said that the paper needed payment up front to print the ad and of course he didn't notice that bit.

So, no publicity for our big break in December 1961 and the thrill of playing in front of about twenty people meant our parting of the ways with Sam.

12

Ringoing The Changes

September 1981

It's great to have you here Richie. All those years ago, who could have pictured two ordinary Liverpool kids here on Bermuda?

Hardly anybody calls me Richie any more. I keep imagining that I was christened Ringo. It's great to hear the name though, especially from you John.

We'll have to get matching diaries soon – it would be perfect to have you here at the same time as Paul and George.

That would be great; it's been too long. When I joined you guys it was liking having three new brothers. I was an only child remember and that meant a lot to me.

Paul was telling me about your great studio. Can you imagine the four of us recording there? I wouldn't miss the screaming girls and the smell of them wetting themselves.

All those phone calls with you and Paul – the two of you have convinced me about the whole I Ching thing. I've been awake at nights thinking about it and I've even started writing notes to make a timeline.

I have so many junctions in my life where I'd thought "What if that hadn't happened?" I could be working in a factory somewhere instead of living this great life.

How far back did you go?

Way back to when I was a little kid. I've never really told you how ill I was; I could have died at the age of seven. It's like that song of yours – there are places I remember.

Brilliant seventh birthday present - in a coma and being rushed into hospital. My burst appendix infected me and they thought I was a goner.

I can still see that lovely nurse's face. I was being wheeled into the operating theatre and I asked her for a cup of sweet tea.

She told me that she'd get one for me when I came round and she did – ten weeks later! I was in that hospital for a year and went back on my fourteenth birthday. Seven and fourteen – must have broken a couple of mirrors.

I was there for two years. I guess treatment for chest stuff has moved on since then, but in those days it was all about rest and so-called convalescence.

Then came the amazing I Ching moment which only makes sense when you think of it that way.

We had people coming in trying to keep us occupied. They meant well but learning how to knit and make baskets wasn't my idea of a good time.

Then – wow – this lady came in with a crop of percussion instruments and all of the kids joined in with big rock numbers like Three Blind Mice.

When she went away with her gear I kept on drumming on my bedside table – must have driven everyone else daft, but my then I had the drumming bug and it stayed for life.

That's just the kind of thing that Paul and I have been telling you about – little things that become really significant when you stand back and look at them.

That's just it. I've read a lot of the I Ching book now and numbers are an important part of it all.

So, on my seventh birthday I nearly died, my fourteenth birthday the drums landed on me, and by my twenty first birthday, I was a professional drummer!

Lucky sevens!

At that time, getting a season's contract at Butlin's was a big thing and I thought that being the drummer with Rory Storm and the Hurricanes in Wales was the top of the tree.

And not that long later you were one of us Beatles!

I've not told you before, but that might not have happened if I liked filling out long boring forms.

You what?

Well, the Hurricanes were doing well and we'd been invited back to Butlin's for 1962, but I was itching to do something more.

Rory was always promising big name foreign tours but they never happened. He'd have been happy to keep doing summers at Butlin's for ever but I was dying to travel.

I was dreaming of the USA. It kicked into all of us didn't it. Do you remember all those records the seamen brought back from the USA to Liverpool? In Britain then the music was people like Dickie Valentine who looked and sounded like your dad, but we were listening to rock and blues for the first time.

There was no chance of me getting there with the Hurricanes, so I thought I'd do something about it.

Being a big port like Liverpool, there was an American Consulate in the city – in the Cunard Building right by the Mersey.

I marched in and announced that I wanted to live and work in the States and I thought they'd bite my hand off.

Turns out I needed to prove I had some money and the promise of a job.

I fancied Houston in Texas because I'd seen some great pictures of the place and the music scene there, so I wrote to the Houston Chamber of Commerce, best handwriting, and asked for a list of job vacancies.

I decided to go for a job in a factory and then find something better once I was living there.

All done, I thought, but it wasn't.

They gave me another pile of forms about the size of a phone book.

They wanted to know all about your family and everything you'd done and people you'd known.

I'm sure there was a question asking if my dog had ever been a communist.

Was he?

I wonder what would have happened if I'd have answered "yes."

I just gave in and put the forms on the fire at home.

Somebody at I Ching headquarters must have wanted me in

Hamburg instead of Houston, because the week after I gave up on going to America, Tony Sheridan asked me to join his backing band at the Top Ten Club in Hamburg.

I gave the Hurricanes a day's notice and set off for Heathrow. There's me flying east when I'd been planning to fly west to the States.

I was bricking it as well. It was the first time I'd ever been on a plane.

That's just it Richie. You still have some tongue in cheek about I Ching, but just think about it. You're never ill in hospital, you liked filling out forms – and you'd never have joined the Beatles.

And Pete Best might still have been the drummer with the Beatles.

Don't put yourself through pain about that Richie. There was all kinds of garbage talked about that; us kicking him out because he was a good looker and had all the girls drooling over him.

It was bloody simple – you were a much better drummer and made us sound so much better. Those times you sat in with us when Pete called in sick, and there were a few, we knew you were making a monster difference.

If anything needed proving, which it didn't, you absolutely nailed it on Abbey Road. Last album we did, and I still love Paul's The End. We just loved that day – three of us doing knockout guitar and you delivering a superb drum solo. I think that was the only drum solo you ever recorded - should have done more!

And that last line. Amazing.

In the end the love you take is equal to the love you make.

How good is that?

So, by November 1962, I'm a Beatle in Hamburg instead of playing for the Hurricanes at Butlin's. Bloody hell; here's to you I Ching.

Everything happened that year. In April, before you joined us, everything was looking great and some money was coming in. Neil Aspinall had packed in being an accountant cos he was earning more being our van driver. He could afford to ferry the van to Hamburg and we actually flew there – a hell of a lot quicker than that first time.

We were booked in at the Star Club – a few leagues above for us after Bruno's dump. The place held two thousand and had proper cinema style seats.

We were as high as kites when we landed but had a real shock. Astrid was the first one to meet us off the plane and she was in tears. Stu was dead – he was only 21 – of a brain haemorrhage.

How cruel is that?

His influence is still here with us. Astrid persuaded him to do his hair in the German student style – combed forward instead of looking like a cheap Elvis. We all copied him and that was that.

And just after Stu died, she took a great picture of George and me in our attic. It was superb – in half-light coming through the window – and that became the inspiration for the With the Beatles album cover. As a real artist, Stu would have been proud.

Here Today – John Lennon in the 21st Century

When you came with us to Hamburg, we were starting to get used to a bit of luxury. Instead of a flea pit next to the toilets, we were in a real hotel with our own single rooms – and the Star Club had a top end sound system.

13
While My Guitar...

November 1981

Look at you John. From being a scouse nuisance in Liverpool to lord of the manor in Bermuda!

And look at you George – still like my little brother but a mighty fine musician.

I'm itching to be back here after Christmas when the four of us can get together, but I wanted to see you so bad that I decided on this solo trip.

I'm really glad you came. Do you remember the old days when we could just knock on each other's doors or just bunk off school to hang out and make music? Now there are teams of people trying to match our diaries.

We became used to that really quickly didn't we? From squashing into a van to go to Hamburg to having our trip to India all sorted.

That's what I really wanted to talk about with you. All those phone calls between us since I was turned on to I Ching by Yoko. Paul and Richie really get it now, but you were way ahead of us.

Without you, we never would have gone to the Maharishi's session in Bangor way back in 67. Who would have thought we'd have gone to Wales to start to understand India mysticism.

It seems like another life doesn't it? It hit us hard when we had the news of the death of Brian. There were all the practicalities of trying to run our lives without the Epstein organisational skill, but the fact that such a young guy could be gone so quickly reminded all of us that none of us are here for ever.

And we were well committed to making our Magical Mystery Tour film – it probably did us some good to be busy and take our minds off Brian for a while.

By the time we got to India in February, you had us well convinced that the Maharishi and his transcendental meditation were the way ahead. Much better than drugs!

It was as bit like a travelling circus by the time we arrived in Rishikesh, do you remember?

Wives, girlfriends, loads of music people and an army of reporters. Just what we needed for quiet meditation!

I still don't think you realise what it did for us – and thousands of other people. Before all that, there was a weird image of India being primitive and we didn't realise that their take on the spiritual world was, at the same time, ancient and in tune with the world as it could be.

Huge numbers of people around the world are going out there to learn – and even if they can't get there in person, they are learning new ways of thinking.

The whole guru Maharishi thing wasn't perfect, but it was a mighty creative time for us – look at how much good stuff we wrote while were there.

You remember that Richie went home first, then Paul, and we jacked it in when the tongues started wagging about the

Maharishi.

Some people had the knives out for him and said he was taking advantage of the girls – and the Beatles, to generate publicity for him.

I've apologised to him since, and I think a lot of it was fabricated by jealous people. In the end, though, none of us is perfect, and the heart of the spirituality is still there.

The thing is John that the whole Indian music thing is what's been driving me crazy – something strange happened there and it's only your I Ching theory that makes sense now.

The first time I heard Indian music it hit me like a hammer. It was calling me to a place where I'd been before.

I think I first heard it when were making the Help film. Someone had the idea of that scene in the Indian restaurant and there was a band playing. I just glazed over and somebody asked me if I'd taken something. I hadn't – the Indian music had taken me.

There was a sitar propped up in the corner and I couldn't stop looking at it. I picked it up and stroked it like a long lost friend. That great shape and loads of strings, and the unbelievable sound.

A few days later I bought a sitar for myself and learned some very basic sounds. Do you remember we were looking for something a bit different in the backing of Norwegian Wood and I suggested using some sitar?

I do remember and my considered musical response – are you daft or what George?

Then we tried it and you and the other guys loved it.

It became a real obsession for me and I remember asking David Crosby from the Byrds about it and he told me to listen to this guy called Ravi Shankar.

I bought some of his albums and I was knocked out.

My brain was telling me that there was no way that I could have heard this kind of music before, but my soul knew better.

It wasn't just the sitar either. Ravi had made an album called Raga and it started with a droning tambura. It has five long stainless steel strings and it was being plucked repeatedly and it was hypnotic. These long, lonely notes rolling around the hollow base of the instrument – it was way better than any drug.

Then Ravi comes in on sitar and it spoke to me. The music was like the sea – ebbing and flowing and drawing me in.

Ages after, I was back in Liverpool and talking to some of our old neighbours who were great. One of them said something which amazed me. He'd heard our records with sitar and he told me that it was no surprise that I liked Indian music.

He said that there was always funny music coming out of our house. I'd forgotten how much my mum liked fiddling about with her short wave radio and finding unusual music from all over the place.

So, while she was pregnant with me, she had Indian music playing in the house.

She picked it up from Radio India and had heard somewhere that the smooth sounds would calm her – and me inside her.

Hell, she was well ahead of her time.

Whether it was that, or a previous life, I don't know -but hearing that music in the Help film took me back – and forward.

Once I met Ravi in India it was astounding.

Musically, he tutored me and helped me to understand how Indian music had totally different beats and rhythms to the western kind.

Even more important, he gave so much time and energy in helping me to develop spiritually.

He gave me some texts to read then took me to the Himalayas to meet his guru.

It was eye opening to watch this man who was my teacher kneeling in front of his guru in sincere humility and respect.

He took me to the Ganges too and I really got why Hindus see it as a sacred river. The water flows all the way from the snows on the Himalayas, and just making contact with the cool water is an act of purification.

We watched people who had lost loved ones taking them to the Ganges for cremation and it was awe inspiring. It was more open and public than a western funeral and seemed to give a welcome sense of closure when ashes were cast into the river.

He talked me through the whole philosophy and religion of re-incarnation as well, and it started to make sense.

He told me that my body was a temporary home for my spirit and it was that, and not my fragile body, which was eternal.

And the meditation was life changing. People only scoff at it *until they've tried it. Sitting still and chanting a simple word like "oom" makes no sense and perfect sense.*

We ended up cutting that trip shorter than it should have been. Do you remember that Ravi told us that we should go to Nepal and learn a lot more. We put that off but I'd love to do it one day.

***

Every time I talk to you and Paul and Richie, we come up with this common track; sleepless nights trying to work out how it all happened for the four of us.

I love that line from Yoko that you told me about when you told her that what happened to us was just luck and we were thrown together.

And she told you that you were right about being thrown together – but who, or what, threw us together?

The four of us might have lived our lives doing ok, but never coming together and becoming something really special as a group.

This whole I Ching bit hurts my brain sometimes. It keeps spinning round – what if that didn't happen? What then?

Paul told me something on the phone the other day that hadn't occurred to me before.

The age we are now you don't take that much notice of a few years in age difference, but when were kids at school it meant a lot.

I still feel like the little brother to you three, but when I was at school, Paul was a year above me and I hardly knew him.

I nodded on the bus occasionally and that was it.

Paul was pretty bright at school and did well at his exams. He was good that the school put him for his GCE exams in Spanish and Latin a year early.

He was expected to sail through them both. He passed Spanish fine but failed his Latin.

I don't know if they still do it in schools today, but Paul had to stay in a lower age group for another year to do it again.

He went back for the new school year and hated it at first. At that age, sitting with kids a bit younger feels like being sent back to primary school.

If he'd have passed his daft Latin exam, I might never have got to know him.

I'm still amazed that we got on so well. I was always the dull kid and he was bouncy and chirpy.

It was the guitar that welded us together. Paul was trying to tell you that I was a decent guitarist, but you were seventeen and I was only fourteen, so you didn't want this little kid around.

Do you remember how I ended up doing my audition on the top deck of a bus?

Paul told me to play Raunchy for you – and I did it bloody well. You looked at Paul and then at me and said "You're in."

Audition over – and if Paul had passed his Latin exam, it would never have happened.

14

When I Was Younger, So Much Younger Than Today

January 1982

Happy New Year Yoko; here's to a good one.

And to you John – and to Bermuda – it's been good for us. Keep on using your kitchen notice board – it's been good for making your mind clearer.

I keep calling it the I Ching Thing. It was a great idea of yours to scribble down any little thing I remembered which made a difference to my life.

I really believe now that even the little things mattered.

Why did you put Buddy Holly's name on the board this morning?

I think we got some of it at the time, but I'm just coming to realise how much him being around changed the way we thought.

When Paul and I first heard his songs it really showed us how to do it. We sat and listened to That'll be the Day over and over again, and Paul said that Words of Love taught him what was possible.

They were such simple tunes and honest words, but they were really new and distinctive.

What struck us later was where he came from. It wasn't New York or Los Angeles; it was a little town we'd never heard of. Lubbock in Texas.

People today wouldn't get it, but it showed us that coming from Liverpool instead of London was not going to be any hindrance at all.

The silliest thing is that he became famous while wearing glasses. I didn't know you could do that!

Right from being a kid, I could hardly see without my specs but hated them. The other kids made fun of me and called me four eyes and the rest.

For years, I took them off every chance I had. Especially if there were girls around. For years, I'd read something or whatever then put them straight into my pocket.

I always remember a great story that Paul told me; it still makes me laugh.

When were really young, I'd been to his house and we had a great time writing songs. The time just goes and it was nearly midnight before we knew it.

It was just before Christmas and getting really cold with a bit of snow on the ground. I headed off home and took my specs off as usual, partly cos they were steaming up and also in case there were any girls around of course.

On the corner of Paul's road, I saw something I could hardly believe – on a really cold night, there were a group of people in their front garden – playing cards!

There were a few of them with their heads down concentrating on the cards, so I just kept walking so that they wouldn't look up and deck me for staring at them.

I told Paul about it the next day and he said he was going down his road to take a look for himself the next evening.

When he told me what I'd really seen he was ill laughing.

"They weren't playing cards; it was a model of people at the manger of baby Jesus in a nativity scene, you dozy bastard."

The world has turned though and I've done my bit for the specs wearers of the world.

When I played Gripweed in the How I won the War film, I was wearing the old fashioned National Health glasses that caused me so much grief when I was young.

I just got used to them and now they are bloody trendy! John Lennon glasses even!

See John – it works out – the Universe doesn't make mistakes.

That cryptic note you put on your I Ching board intrigued me – Decca, wrong but right. What does that mean?

That's a good one. There was a guy called Dick Rowe who became world famous for turning down the Beatles before it all kicked off for us. He was right though – we didn't sound that good at the time. And what a time.

By then, after a few false starts, we had a proper manager in Brian Epstein. He impressed the parents, and even Aunt Mimi, because he looked like a real gentleman in his smart suit and sounded like one with his posh voice.

He'd latched on to us because people were going in to his record shop and asking for our record – and he'd never heard of us. Then he came down into the Cavern and something caught him.

George always said that it was a good match because we needed somebody to lift us out of the cellar and Eppy needed something to bring him down to normal life.

To be fair, he was working his socks off to get us more money and tried to get us in front of a record company.

Not many of them would consider anything north of London, though, and he was turned down flat by the big guys like HMV and Columbia.

Decca seemed interested though and they actually sent a guy to watch us at the Cavern.

We were chuffed to bits when they booked us for an audition in London on the daftest possible date – January 1st, 1962.

Instead of partying on New Year's Eve, we went down to London in a hired van.

The first bit of the M1 motorway had only been open for a few months, and, of course, it didn't go to anywhere near Liverpool.

It was snowing and we got lost twice somewhere in the Midlands, so it was after nine 'o'clock in the evening before we arrived.

Brian had gone down on the train, first class of course, but we had to take all our gear like instruments and big amplifiers.

We met Brian for a meal then took a look in Trafalgar Square to see drunks in the fountain celebrating the New Year – it made Liverpool look normal.

The whole look of London threw us really. We'd felt like big fishes at home but now we were little tiddlers in the big city.

Looking back, it was no surprise that Decca turned us down. Brian knew business but he didn't know the popular music game then. The set list we did was middle of the road and wrong. We didn't play the stuff that had audiences rocking in Hamburg and Liverpool.

They thought were an amateur outfit as well because we'd lugged down all our big amplifiers in the van. They had everything set up in the studio so we didn't even use them.

What happened next was pure I Ching – and it wouldn't have come about if Decca had taken us on.

When Eppy was trying to get a contract for us he was carrying around a heavy reel to reel tape recorder. It probably looked amateurish as well because most people brought demo records.

He found out that he could get his tapes turned into records above the HMV shop in Oxford Street in London, so off he went to get that done.

And here's the thing which only makes sense when I think of someone up there at I Ching control room bringing in an ordinary guy to change our world.

The man who was doing the pretty routine job of cutting the discs pricked up his ears when he heard the songs we'd written ourselves.

He asked Brian if they'd ever been published, which they hadn't. And so, this disc cutter Jim suggests that Brian heads to the floor above to see a guy called Syd who was in charge of EMI's publishing company Ardmore and Beechwood.

He liked the stuff we'd written too, and, his business brain kicking in quickly, Eppy said that, if he could help in getting the Beatles a recording contract, then Ardmore and Beechwood could have the publishing rights.

That really made the difference. We'd made ourselves into a tight and polished group by doing great covers of the rock classics, but our own songs were what made us different.

It became even better when George Martin became involved. Without Decca turning us down, we'd never have met him and he made just about the biggest ever contribution to making us successful.

He was only thirty six but he was head of Parlophone Records. They were a part of EMI but George didn't have a recording artist who could sell to the youth market.

Other parts of the company had people like Cliff Richard selling a lot of records and George needed to catch up.

He was a classically trained musician and he told me later that he knew next to nothing about pop music. He didn't even get why Elvis was popular.

When Eppy turned up at his office with his new demo records of us his ears pricked up. He liked what he heard and was impressed that the publishing company were keen as well.

He took his time to make up his mind, but, by May, Eppy sent us a telegram to Hamburg.

I still have it.

CONGRATULATIONS BOYS. Stop
EMI REQUEST RECORDING SESSION. Stop
PLEASE REHEARSE NEW MATERIAL

We were dancing around like daft kids.

Do you know John; I'm going to start a new career for you as a conference speaker about I Ching.

Just look at that set of happenings. Not coincidences. You get your audition wrong, so Decca turn you down. A simple disc cutter spots your song writing talent, and you now have the dream team of Brian Epstein and George Martin on your side. If one cog of that had not clicked in you wouldn't be here today.

You are so right. We were a perfect fit with George Martin, He knew nowt about rock'n'roll music and we knew the lot, but he knew everything about other kinds of music. We taught him a lot, but he taught us a lot more.

15

Starting Over

May 1985

What's amusing you in your morning paper Yoko; you have a helluva smile on your face.

Do you remember a bit back John when I told you that I was going to start your new career as a conference speaker? Now here you are twice in next week's listings about coming attractions in Bermuda.

And the best bit – this might sound ungrateful, but neither one is about music nor the Beatles. It's just me in a new life.

At one of my talks last month a guy asked me if I could play guitar! He only knew me as a speaker and discussion leader around here. I like that. I've not given up on music or writing it, and I never will, but that's just part of what I do now, not all of it.

I feel as though I have a great balance now. I love sitting in the Swizzle Bar on Front Street chatting about everything and nothing. And I can sip one of those swizzles for ages. I can enjoy an occasional drink, without using it to wipe me out.

There were times in the past where I needed a bottle of whisky or more to write, but not now.

I still get shivers when I think about that "lost weekend" of mine which lasted months. I'd stayed away from you and I had no guide.

I wrote Cold Turkey in 1969 and it was the most dismal, depressing song every. The other Beatles wanted nothing to do with it and they were dead right. When we released it as a Plastic Ono song it crept into the lower end of the charts which was more than it deserved.

The way I am now is down to you Yoko. It sounds so simple but it took you to convince me that I could be whatever I wanted to be. I didn't have to keep turning out a product that other people wanted from me. If I wanted to be a househusband, or a student of history, or do nothing at all, it was up to me.

You still have the writer's gift though – creating interest. Those two talks listed would make lots of people want to come, including me – I Ching and Bermuda, and Shakespeare on Bermuda. Really attention grabbing.

What I like best is that you aren't just talking, you are listening too.

Now that I'm well plugged in to life here, I'm amazed at how many interesting people live in Bermuda – and how much I didn't know.

That series of talks on the teachings of the Buddha left me mesmerised and I've now read just about everything he ever wrote.

He was around centuries before Jesus Christ, and that guy said some good stuff too. I wish I'd said that before that interview about the Beatles being bigger than him. It might have saved some bonfires of our stuff in the States.

You are right about that blend John. My mother was a

Buddhist and my father was a Christian so I got all that. It's like most religions if you look at the basics – many more similarities than differences. I'm always amazed at how many wars and feuds are based on religion. If they just listened to each other it wouldn't happen.

Buddha had some great lines – I kept humming tunes to go with them and I feel a new album coming on.

I feel so good that I've melted away any anger I had with past differences with Paul and George and Ringo. They seem so trivial now. Just think, if that creature had shot me back in 1980, I'd have died with too much unrepaired.

There's a great Buddha line that says, "holding on to anger is like drinking poison and expecting the other person to die."

Perfectly put John. So, how are you going to link I Ching and Bermuda in your talk?

Well, I want to kick off with a few key points that you alerted me to, but I don't want to lecture – I want to open up minds and encourage people to learn for themselves, just like I did.

Bermuda's story is a perfect example though. I hadn't realised that almost forever nobody lived here. It wasn't like the Caribbean or North America where there were native populations for centuries before the Europeans arrived to kick them out or subjugate them.

It fascinated me to look at the maps of the routes that people like Christopher Columbus and Magellan took to come from Europe in search of new lands.

They were mighty brave to head west and hope to find land. No satellites in those days and, of course, Columbus thought he had gone round the world and found India when he landed in the Caribbean.

Darker skin and strange language, so it must be India.

What's really interesting is the routes they took which worked best with currents and prevailing winds.

Both routes were well away from Bermuda so none of them saw it.

Then, in 1609, I Ching did its thing and a ship landed here accidentally.

The Sea Venture had about 150 settlers on board heading to start a new life in Jamestown, Virginia and the ship hit a storm – I know how they must have felt from my adventure.

There was a fleet of nine which had set off from Plymouth in England but Sea Venture had become separated and lost.

This was a pretty simple wooden ship and it was in great danger of sinking. What happened next is often described as a shipwreck, but it wasn't. Credit to the captain when he realised he was way off course but saw the waves crashing onto a reef ahead.

He deliberately steered to it and the ship stuck so that his passengers and crew could get off and reach the safety of land.

And that land was Bermuda.

The guy in charge was Admiral Sir George Somers and I'd have liked him. All on board lived safely and managed to exist on what they found, including a great herd of pigs.

The still wanted to get to Jamestown though and what they did next was amazing.

The took the wreckage of Sea Venture and, along with some Bermuda cedar, built two new ships, the Deliverance and the Patience.

The used the rigging from Sea Venture and had ships good enough to travel the 600 miles or so west to the mainland.

We've seen that brilliant replica of Deliverance in St George's just next to the main square. I've passed it dozens of times but went inside for the first time last week. It feels really small and cramped inside but it worked.

The local guide expert took me for a walk to Alexandra Battery Beach and right next to it is Building Bay Beach.

That's the exact spot where they built Deliverance and Patience; no shipyards or modern gear, just ingenuity and hard work.

Before they started their journey, they left behind just two men to retain ownership of the island for England.

They set off on May 10th, 1610, and made it to Jamestown but had a mighty shock. Only about fifty of the five hundred settlers on the main fleet had survived with most of them dying of starvation.

Soon after, George Somers took the Patience back to Bermuda to bring food but he took ill on the way.

He died in Bermuda and, as he stated in his will, his heart was buried here and his body sent back to England. What a man.

I wonder what would have happened to Bermuda if your I Ching guys had not made the Sea Venture hit that reef at St George's. It could have been a Spanish ship that found the island and everyone here would have been speaking Spanish instead of English.

Or how about a German ship and we'd all have been speaking kraut! It would be just like being back in bloody Hamburg.

That's really going to grab the attention around here John, and I love the idea of relating I Ching to where people live. A lot of that is new to me John, but how do you link Bermuda with Shakespeare? He never came here surely?

16

Shall I Compare Thee To The Twilight Zone?

You are right Yoko; he never came here but he did know about us. Shakespeare died in 1616 but he did hear about the discovery of Bermuda in 1609.

Even without newspapers or internet, news travelled pretty quicky in a big trading centre like London and everybody was talking about the wreck of the Sea Venture and the new land it had accidentally discovered and, of course, claimed for the British Empire.

About a year or so after the news emerged, Shakespeare wrote The Tempest, one of his last solo plays and considered to be one of his best.

It's based on a shipwreck, but not just any shipwreck. There are so many similarities between Shakespeare's play and what those who landed in 1609 said that the case is just about certain.

The characters in the Tempest, like those who landed from the wreck of Sea Venture, spoke of the pigs, the noises at night from wildlife, and, in the absence of beer, drinking a concoction made from berries.

It's not just Shakespeare's stories though is it John? There's something else there.

You are so right Yoko, and something really odd really punched itself into my head. Years ago, when I could, I loved watching a TV series called The Twilight Zone and it was brilliant.

It was really mind stretching and most episodes left you wondering for ages afterwards. There was one episode, and I wish I could find it again, which had a brilliant central idea which said that some of the greatest minds in history had all been the same person – Shakespeare, Leonardo da Vinci, Einstein, Isaac Newton and the rest.

They'd all been re-incarnated or whatever.

And what if you were one of them John?

I wouldn't have dared to say this at one time, but I thought I was a genius from being a kid.

I was staggered that nobody had noticed. Then I read somewhere that there's a fine line between being mad and being a genius. Well, nobody had locked me up so perhaps I was a genius.

I wondered why all the other people at school, kids and teachers, were so thick and perhaps they were afraid of me cos I was a genius.

Even my Aunt Mimi didn't get it. I gave her all my brilliant poems and she threw them in the bin. I told her she'd regret it when I was famous.

Being a genius is hard work though and some days I just fancied being a carpenter or a fisherman where I could do a day's work and then just switch off.

Being a genius is a full time job I can tell you.

So, are you seeing the same genius signs in Buddha and Shakespeare?

Absolutely yes Yoko.

I could read you some of their great lines and you'd be hard put to guess which of them it came from.

It might sound arrogant, but it reminds me of Paul and myself at our song writing best. We could write hit songs to order, or more profound stuff as we matured.

If Buddha and Shakespeare could ever sit together, I would imagine them trading lines like that.

Shakespeare saying, from The Tempest -

We are such stuff as dreams are made on and our little life is ended with a sleep.

And Buddha coming back with –

In the end, only three things matter; how much you loved, how gently you lived, and how gracefully you let go of things not meant for you.

I remember that Paul and I said pretty much the same, but less elegantly, when we wrote We Can Work it Out together - "Life is very short and there's no time for fussing and fighting my friend."

There's no harm at all in learning from the past John, but remember what Lord Buddha said:

The secret of health for both mind and body is not to mourn for the past, nor to worry about the future, but to live the present moment wisely and earnestly.

My mother always said that it was really important to read his words carefully and find the full meaning. Buddha didn't say ignore the past, he said don't mourn it, and he didn't say don't think about the future, he said don't worry about it.

The main advice is to live the present moment. Carpe diem, they say don't they, seize the day.

As Buddha said, "Every morning we are born again. What we do today is what matters most."

I've left my writings of Buddha open at his first universal truth.

"Nothing is lost in this universe. Old solar systems disintegrate into cosmic rays. We are the children of our parents and we will be the parents of our children."

My mother always quoted that line, and my father said it was like the Christian funeral service: "Ashes to ashes, dust to dust."

I thought about those lines when I saw those incredible cremations at the River Ganges. The soul living on and the shell of the used body going back to its source.

It says it all, doesn't it? From Buddhism, Christianity and Hinduism – three almost identical profound thoughts about the meaning of the soul's life and bodily death.

Do you know John, that session we attended in Hamilton on Gaia Theory has been playing on my mind too.

Could it be possible that the whole planet is part of all this too?

I'm starting to believe it's all possible thought it sounded crazy when I first heard about it. Then again, a lot of stuff we've done had the same reaction.

The fact that a lot of the establishment figures are rubbishing the Gaia concept make me like it more, not less.

That central idea of the Earth itself interacting with organisms and us to achieve a balance fascinates me.

I know there's a lot of the Universe to explore, but the Gaia idea that something is self-regulating our planet to make it home for us strikes a chord with me. We've found nowhere else it's happened yet.

How the climate works, most of the time, and how seawater keeps a constant level of salinity baffles the scientists and even they admit that they don't understand the whole picture.

The idea that made all the jaws drop at that session was that, if humans stop being part of the balance, Gaia could remove us from the planet. Perhaps we deserve that.

I love the idea that the whole theory is named after the Greek goddess Gaia who represented the soul of the Earth in their mythology.

Isn't it great that all of the religions and the great cultures have been searching for whatever truth is beyond us?

I keep a very open mind.

Shakespeare did it again – "There are more things in heaven and earth than are dreamt of in your philosophy."

Perfectly put.

17
Back To Bed?

May 1986

This is turning into a weird year Yoko. That disaster last month in Chernobyl is frightening me: whatever went wrong at that nuclear plant is going to have an impact on thousands of people. The fallout won't touch us here in Bermuda, but most of Europe is scared stiff. Just imagine if something like that happened in the States.

At least it's reminding people that national borders don't mean a thing – an artificial line is not going to help if something that bad happens on such a big scale.

When this year started it felt like big things were happening. I still have the awful pictures in my head of what happened to the Challenger Shuttle back in January. Imagine the nightmare of all the hard preparation, the thrill of blast off, then, 73 seconds later, your life is over.

Do you remember before that all went wrong, we were wrapped up in one of its missions being to find out more about Halley's Comet?

We were lucky to have that guy in Bermuda who did the series of talks about it, and I devoured every book and bit of film I could find.

I was amazed to find that the comet had been seen since way back in 240 BC. It took until 1705 for that guy Halley to work out that it was visible to Earth every 75 years or so. All of the experts told him he was wrong and that couldn't be true, but he had all the evidence and he was dead right.

When you look back through historical documents, it keeps popping up on that cycle – it's even in the Bayeux Tapestry recording the Norman invasion of England in 1066.

It's no surprise that people thought that its appearance meant that something major would be happening on our planet.

The smart guys scoff at that but who knows? "There are more things in heaven and earth …."

It blows my mind to think of that ball of dust and ice travelling on its huge orbit all alone. Just think, it won't be back here until about 2061.

We won't see it John, but we'll join it in being part of the Universe by then.

That's the perfect way to think about ending this life. The more I've learned about religions, the good bits, the more accepting I can be. I know I talked about "imagine no religion" but it would have been too long a line for the song if I'd have written "imagine no religion, well the bad bits anyway, but the good parts that teach you about our place in the Universe make perfect sense". The line wouldn't scan much.

You are funny John, and you can smile at yourself; you've lost that edge that made you use your humour to be aggressive and cruel to people.

That's down to you Yoko. I think I got it right in Woman –

"I will try to express

My inner feeling and thankfulness

For showing me the meaning of success"

Thank you sir.

I don't mourn the past, honestly, but I do keep thinking about what happened at the Dakota way back in 1980.

That poor lookalike guy who died when it should have been me. Being selfish, if I had died that day I would have gone unprepared. I'm not looking forward to death but I don't fear it now – it does feel like stepping into another part of a natural evolution.

I remember an old friend from Liverpool who was one of the bravest men I ever met.

Billy was way fitter than any of us and he went on to play top level football. Then, just after he stopped playing, he was hit by motor neurone disease.

It's one of the cruellest conditions ever. He said it was like your body shutting down around you while your mind stayed razor sharp. Towards the end his wife and his carer had to do literally everything for him.

His voice was weakening too, but I sat and had a long talk with him one evening and he told me he was lucky.

Lucky!

He told me about a friend of his, Kenny, who had died the year before. He'd been coming home by taxi from a late night out and it was such a lovely evening that he asked the driver to drop him at the end of his road so that he could have a blast of fresh air before bed.

He was probably too relaxed and got out of the car on the

driver's side instead of wriggling over to the safer option of the pavement.

Then this drunken idiot came along at high speed and hit Kenny and the car door, killing the poor guy instantly.

Billy said that Kenny died without any warning, but he felt lucky because he'd had a few years' notice of his own death.

He had time to tell people he loved them and in "tidy his life up."

God, that's real courage.

That really moved me John. Do you think it's time for us to try to make a difference again?

You are reading my mind. I was wondering whether the world needs another bed in?

It really does, and it needs to be reminded that we are one world, one people. Chernobyl should be a smack in the face to learn that.

I'm smiling because I'm thinking back to 1969 when we did our first bed in for peace. It was a different world then and I was a different me.

You were telling me that we didn't need to get married and everything was fine as it was. I nagged and nagged until you agreed. It was totally different to when I married Cynthia all those years ago. She was a lovely woman, but I got it all wrong.

I'd made her pregnant and back then "you had to get married" to do the decent thing.

I just about had to hide her away because our manager Eppy told us that pop stars had to look single and available to attract the girls. He was probably right, and I didn't need much persuading as I was enjoying the bachelor life anyway.

You were fixing our wedding like a dog with a bone; you wouldn't let it go. Do you remember all the ideas you tried?

Of course! Everything from an ocean liner to a cross channel ferry. We didn't want it to be in England because we'd have had a circus of reporters and cameras. It had to be somewhere British though because I'm English and you had the Japanese passport.

It was a friend who suggested Gibraltar which I'd never thought of it, and it was perfect.

It's a lot like Bermuda if you think about it – very British in style and feeling like home in England.

It was even more symbolic than we knew because people centuries ago saw it as the end of the world – they didn't know that there was anything west across the Atlantic – certainly not Bermuda!

Typical us though – for most people the honeymoon is a private time away from people, but we invited the world to join in!

Married on March 20th and a few days later we're at the Amsterdam Hilton from the 25th to the 31st and we told the press that they could come anytime between nine in the morning till nine at night to ask questions.

We did the right thing though. We'd become performance artists and we could use our fame to get people there. It was a lot more powerful than a thousand speeches by politicians.

Nixon had just become the US President and was making

promises about ending the war in Vietnam. They'd been talking for months about the peace talks in Paris and had got as far as trying to agree on the shape of the bloody meeting table!

Those talks were grinding along while people were being killed every day. We did more with our week in bed than the genius politicians did in months.

Of course, we wanted to move straight on to do another bed session in New York, but that cannabis conviction against you meant that you couldn't enter the States at that time.

We ended up in Montreal in Canada, about as close as we could get and we were still grabbing world attention – talking and singing about peace at the end of May 69 at the Fairmont Queen Elizabeth Hotel. Sounds British again!

That war in Vietnam went on till 1975, but we had the world talking about the stupidity of it all and I'm sure we made a difference. And that song of yours was sung by millions of people around the world – Give Peace a Chance.

Even stubborn politicians couldn't ignore that.

Something else struck me about that song too.

Do you remember all those sessions I attended about Shakespeare and his writing?

That joke I was making about my "imagine no religion" line needing to scan?

All those years I was writing Beatles songs with Paul, we could feel what scansion meant but we didn't know much more.

It was like the music – we needed George Martin to take us

up to a better level of musical understanding.

And now my literature group in Bermuda are getting me to understand words better too – and it's not bad having Shakespeare as a mentor either!

I'd never heard of iambic pentameter, but I'd been using it for years without realising it.

Tell me more John.

It's really simple, but clever and complicated at the same time. You have to hear it and feel it rather than read it. It reminds me of when Ravi Shankar was showing George and me how to play the sitar and understand Indian music. It's so different to western rhythms, but once you get it, it really clicks.

Iambic pentameter just means a line with five pairs of syllables, with those syllables alternately stressed and unstressed.

As you say, simple!

Like learning Indian music, it's best to tap your fingers on the table and let it flow.

You know that brilliant eighteenth sonnet by Shakespeare, the one you love?

Shall I compare thee to a summer's day?

That's the one. Now say it slowly and tap your fingers to the rhythm.

Got it. That's good.

It kind of grabs the attention too. The technique goes way back to the Greeks but Shakespeare really was a master.

Do you remember when we went see Romeo and Juliet? The very first line of the play?

"Two households both alike in dignity."

Tap your fingers through it and see what I mean?

That's amazing. Like I'm hearing the words for the first time.

And when we were sitting on the bed in Montreal and came up with "All we are saying is give peace a chance."

Wow, that works too!

Iambic pentameter and I didn't even know I was doing it!

Perhaps it's why huge crowds all over the world were singing it as a peace anthem. If you add one syllable to that line it loses a lot of power.

Looking back, you know, I was a bit dismissive of people who saw classical themes in the songs that Paul and I were writing.

I dug out this cutting from The Times newspaper the other day and, at the time, I laughed at it.

Their guy was actually full of praise for what we were doing, but I was too arrogant to notice.

Listen to this –

Lennon and McCartney have grasped back the lead for British based music after years of our pop groups copying what comes out of the United States. They obviously think of harmony and melody simultaneously and effortlessly build major tonic sevenths and ninths into their tunes. They use flat submediant key switches and at the end of their Not a

Second Time tune is a perfect Aeolian cadence. That was the same chord progression at the end of Mahler's Song of the Earth.

We were too full of ourselves to listen to much else, but I'm more receptive now. I actually found a company called a cuttings agency and they did a search for musical experts writing about us in the press over the years. I paid them to send me anything they found and I was expecting something shoe box size but it was a huge trunk full when it arrived!

I'm still going through them but I found a superb piece about the sheer quantity of songs that Paul and I wrote.

This top music professor said that our output was up there with great composers like Schubert and Mozart. They both wrote about seven hundred songs each, just like we did. He rated us as even better because many of ours were top rated and we had a much better quality ratio than those two. We weren't bad were we?

That musical magic can still make a massive difference. We can multiply what Give Peace a Chance and bed ins did a million times over.

Let's have a think and take some advice – the world has moved on a helluva lot since we did all that. I'm getting better at listening to other people and I'll do it big time.

18

Here There and Everywhere

September 1987

We've done well in this last year or so to take some advice and have a good look round before diving into something too soon.

The world is a different place since our bed ins and we might need to do things differently.

I feel confident and happy about the future but I can smile about the past too.

That Help song I wrote way back in 1965 is still special to me; I still like it cos it was so honest, me talking about how I felt –

When I was younger, so much younger than today
I never needed anybody's help in any way
But now those days are gone, I'm not so self-assured
Now I find I've changed my mind; I've opened up the doors.

That Help movie we made wasn't the best work we ever did, but every time I think of it, I smile about the money.

It was starting to get into hard work with all the paperwork and legal stuff and the financial experts.

They were trying to explain it to us, we were pretty innocent and naïve then.

We seemed to have a lot of money on paper, but I asked

them where it actually was and I was told a lot of it was in the Bahamas for tax reasons.

The other guys laughed out loud when I came up with a great question – can we go and see it then?

That was only a few years after playing tiny venues and counting every penny – now we are mega rich and making a film while counting our money in the Bahamas.

It wasn't just the four of us who were the innocents with money. For all his business sense, Eppy got well stuffed early on.

We were all so thrilled with being a success in the States that we didn't even know that dealers there were making enormous money from us. We were so chuffed to see all the posters and souvenirs with our names and photos on them that it never struck us that someone was making a mint, and it wasn't us.

The record deals we were getting were crap too and we've lost millions out of that over the years.

It was the main reason we punished ourselves with non-stop touring and it was no longer much fun. Non-stop travel and trapped in posh hotel rooms with fans screaming outside.

Part of the reason for the big stadium gigs was the police – they didn't want us playing in a venue for a thousand people if it meant another twenty thousand fans causing a riot outside.

Those big venues were bringing in big money to make up for the tiny revenue from record sales.

So many bands are doing big stadium gigs now, but we did it

first.

When we did Shea Stadium in New York it was staggering; I thought we'd reached the top of the mountain. Playing in a small venue was more fun cos everyone could hear us, including us. We were looking at each other and especially Richie for the beat because we couldn't hear a thing because of the screaming and being a long way from the audience.

Hell – 55.600 people there and most of them must have enjoyed actually seeing us live but they can't have heard much.

Big stadium venues have great sound systems now but Shea's was awful. Vox made us some huge amplifiers but most of the sound was coming through the stadium's public address system which was mainly used for announcing team news at sporting events!

The ticket sales were making us a fortune every night we did one of those.

The very last stadium event we did was in August 1966 at Candlestick Park in San Francisco. Just to prove that even some Americans can be bad at business, the organisers lost money on that one. We made our $100.000 as in the contract, but they didn't even fill the place. Took some doing by the organisers, losing money on a Beatles gig in the Sixties.

At the end of the show, they bundled us into this steel truck and we bounced around in it while they got us out of the place. Big stars – right – in a bare cattle truck!

It was a cold and foggy night and that didn't help, but we all knew that it was the end of an era. By the time we got back to London we knew that this was it. Getting into the studio and making good stuff was a million times better than nights like Candlestick Park.

People kept nagging us to get on tour again but why would we? We were really enjoying studio life and creating good music instead of being dancing puppets in the middle of a sports field.

The year after that showed how fast the world and technology was changing. Even before we did our bed ins, television was becoming like the science fiction ideas from when I was a kid – being able to see live pictures from another country.

It was stunning at the time; singing All You Need is Love in front of so many people in 1967 - they reckon that over four hundred million people saw that live in about twenty five countries. Eppy said it was our finest moment.

Don't know about that but it was awesome.

When you think about those global viewers, we might need to re-think how we do a bed in for the world today.

Those media consultants we spoke to still think that the general principle is right. Getting the attention and making people talk about giving peace a chance.

As they say, it's like advertising. Peace is our product and we can use the same techniques to sell it. Even if we get an unfriendly paper using a headline saying that they think our idea is rubbish – at least the idea is out there.

Those numbers keep leaping up don't they? It staggered you when you had over fifty thousand people at Shea Stadium, then felt ballistic when you had over four hundred million watching you singing All You Need is Love on the Our World TV show.

Then the Live Aid show you and Paul did a couple of years ago capped the lot!

It's true. I thought tens of thousands at Wembley in London and the JFK Stadium in Philadelphia at the same time was astounding, but the TV figures! They estimated nearly two billion watching worldwide. That's almost half of the planet's population.

And Bob Geldof was right. It didn't solve the poverty problem but it sure as hell put it on government agendas. He said that rock'n'roll was the language that unified the world's conscience, not English.

The money side of events like that gets worse. All those huge events; the artists get nowt but millions go to the organisers, the trucks, the sound systems, the venues, and so on and so on.

You know how it is. We get dozens of letters every week from well-meaning people who want us to "simply" put on a concert for their pet cause.

I'm glad we've taken time to take stock and work with people to come up with a better and fairer way of doing all that. For the moment, the fact that we give ten per cent of our income to good causes works. It's just like the very old religious idea of a "tithe" on your earnings for people who need the help, and it's not a bad idea.

Let's stand back a while and decide what the world needs and what we want to do.

19
New York City

January 19th, 1994

Good evening distinguished guests, ladies and gentlemen. Welcome to the Waldorf Astoria, welcome to a great city, and, in particular, welcome to one of the biggest events in music; our induction of new members of the Rock and Roll Hall of Fame.

It's a particular honour for us all that John Lennon is joining a very distinguished list tonight, and, to induct him, will you please welcome the one and only – Paul McCartney.

Thank you so much and I'm actually nervous with John and his wife Yoko sitting in front of me, but here goes.

I've been wondering for ages how to do this, but John always said that I was good at writing letters, so here's one I've written to you John.

As I write this letter to send my love to you...

I kicked it off with some memories of playing together at a little village party in Woolton in Liverpool. Do you remember you started that day playing a cheap guitar on the back of a lorry? It had better sound than Shea Stadium though.

And how about our song writing? It was mainly at my house, well my dad's house, or your mum's house. We took it for granted that we could do it but someone up there had put us together to do something special. Do you remember we made cigarettes out of Typhoo tea leaves from the kitchen? It smelt foul and didn't do a thing for us, but we thought we looked cool.

Thinking about it, we should have stuck to Typhoo in later years.

We became really cool when you had that hundred pounds from a rich relative in Edinburgh and we decided to go and see Europe. I was dead impressed – a hundred quid for a 21st birthday present! I knew I was working class compared to you being posh and middle class, but a gift like that made me think you were royalty.

It was a lot of money then and you were generous and said we should both go on holiday with it.

I laughed out loud when you recorded Working Class Hero later on. I suppose a song called I'm Posh wouldn't have been a hit.

Somebody told us that we'd get better results from drivers while you were hitching lifts if you had a gimmick, so we wore bowler hats – and it worked.

We meant to get as far as Spain but loved Paris and stayed there. We chatted and learned a lot – and had our hair cut. The student style was hair combed forward like Astrid had done with Stu in Hamburg.

When we went home to Liverpool people thought we looked daft, but it worked in the end didn't it?

We did our own thing didn't we? Do you remember playing at the Cavern and being told it was a jazz club? We kept getting notes sent up on stage from the boss telling us to cut out the rock and roll.

I remember you looking me in the eye and keeping a straight face when you announced a jazz number called Wake up Little Susie.

I know we all look back with affection on the days when we were poor but travelling back from a gig in an old van with a broken windshield was special. It was freezing cold and we piled on top of each other in the back to keep warm. A Beatles sandwich!

Later on, we met Elvis in California and my biggest memory is that he had the first TV remote control we'd ever seen.

And, fast forward, I remember Yoko coming to see me looking for a music manuscript and then she went to see you.

And we get on well despite all the garbage you read. We are like a family and all families have the odd bust up, but love brings them back together.

I've talked too long John, but thanks to Yoko for giving me something special to end my session. You don't know a thing about this, but she gave me a demo you did at home in the Dakota back in 1977. Just you and a piano, and, I hope you like it, I've added a bit to it – pass the guitar please.

Whatever happened to the life that we once knew]

Can we really live without each other

Where did we lose the touch

That seemed to mean so much

It always made me feel - free as a bird.

Thank you Paul. I promised I wouldn't cry tonight, but you just made me do it.

John Lennon. You have made it – you are in the Rock and Roll Hall of Fame.

20

Tomorrow Never Knows

October 9th, 2000

A very happy 60th birthday John – you made it.

It's a surprise isn't it. When I was 40 I was waiting for life to begin as promised, but it already had. They reckon that 60 is the new 40 so here we go again.

It must be your I Ching teaching again but isn't it funny how a throwaway remark can set you thinking.

When Paul did that top speech for me at the Rock and Roll Hall of Fame induction there was one thing in particular that sat in my head.

He was right to make fun of me for writing Working Class Hero cos I wasn't. I lived in very comfortable semi-detached house and a lot of my relatives had good jobs. He was right – working class kids didn't get a hundred pounds for a birthday present.

Paul, George and Richie were much more working class and I wanted to be more like them. Then again, so did most of Britain in the Sixties – people who had been to expensive schools and spoke like the Queen tried using a Liverpool accent to sound trendy.

It made me really think about working class kids and the chances they don't get. The four of us were lucky, or thrown together by I Ching, and I wonder how many talented kids will never get that chance, whether they are from Liverpool or anywhere else in the world.

It was a great idea of yours to sit down in private with people we could talk to. Not people looking to get anything from us but people who knew what it was like to have a lot of money and wonder how best to use it.

Once you have a great house and all the luxuries, there really is a responsibility to do something right.

Once we set up the Lennon Foundation, it fell into place – people we could trust looking after the finance and the legals and we could concentrate on what was important to us.

Let's split our noticeboard in half and keep adding your I Ching notes on one side, and use the other space for a list of your key tasks you want to do.

We'll leave that "to do" list on the board until you've achieved them.

So – what's going on that list?

Bed ins – still up there. We should go back to Amsterdam and Montreal and see what's changed. They can be broadcast live worldwide and we'll see what effect it has. We can make them interactive too and work with that.

Sailing for kids – now I've got that started, I want to make it bigger and stronger. Most kids in Liverpool look at the river and the sea most days but never get to use it. The kids we've had through the programme already are changed by it. It's not just learning how a sailboat works, it's having the responsibility and lives in your hands. I love the fact that quite a few of them are working as instructors now.

It hadn't occurred to me before, but the television guys love the idea and want to take it further. They want to film the kids sailing the boat from Rhode Island to Bermuda as a I did and want to go for the really big one – travelling in the path of Leif Erikson when he came from Scandinavia to America a thousand years ago.

They think it will all make great TV and they can do it all live with modern equipment. Their best idea is a beauty. They want to create a wreck – identical to the Sea Venture that hit the reef in Bermuda -and see if a modern group could do what the original settlers did. Using only tools of the time, they will aim to use the reclaimed wood to build two ships and sail them to Jamestown Virginia.

Children's books – I'd still like to write books for kids. When I was young I loved books like Alice in Wonderland for taking me into my own world. I didn't understand until much later that Lewis Carroll was using a kids' book to comment on what was wrong with the world. It was the foundation for my I Am the Walrus, but I got it wrong – I read the book again and realised that the walrus was the bad guy. Then again, I Am the Carpenter wouldn't have worked would it?

I'd love to write books for kids that makes learning fun, but really drives them to get to know about the world. I'd like them to be good enough for adults to enjoy too – never talk down to kids. I think I might make my main character a cat so that kids can really take to him. That's a neat idea.

Here's the security guy again John. It must have taken most of his day to scan all the birthday cards and gifts that came for you. This package is heavy, but he says they've triple scanned and x rayed it and it's fine.

Way of the world I guess to have security checking birthday wishes but it keeps the crazies away!

This heavy one feels like a brick! It is a brick, with a note from Paul.

I don't know if you should feel your eyes filling up at my great age, but they are.

The brick is from the original Cavern in Liverpool. If only walls had ears says Paul, they could tell some tales.

There's gold lettering around the sides of the brick. Looks like lyrics from a song but I don't recognise the words.

Listen to this – beautiful message from Paul.

"Way back in December 1980, the message came through about the fatal shooting outside your Dakota building. The first reports were confused and one said that it was you that had been killed.

All I could think to do was go into my room and be by myself. And I did what we always did together – I picked up a guitar and wrote a song – to you.

It was a great moment when we heard that you were ok - by then, I'd written the song and I'm pleased as hell I never needed to sing it as a memorial to you my great friend.

I've changed the words a bit and they are on the brick. I hope they make sense to you.

Here Today – John Lennon in the 21st Century

What about the time we met
Well, I suppose you could say
That we were playing hard to get
Didn't understand a thing
But we could always sing
I really love you and I'm glad that you came along
I'm so happy that you are here today.

―――――――――――――

Look out for the sequel to Here Today ...continuing the life of John Lennon from 2000 to the present day.

Credits

This book has been forty years in the making and I'd like to warmly thank so many people who have shared stories and insights with me. Just listening amid great company around the world gave me all I needed whether it was in Liverpool, Hamburg, Amsterdam or Bermuda.

In particular I'd like to thank –

All at Michael Terence Publishing

Gerry Marsden

Mike Pender

Sam Leach

Astrid Kircherr

Valerie Radetzky, Paul Kolnik and Corinne Samios in New York

Epstein House, Liverpool

Gosling's of Bermuda

Oceania Cruises

Karolina Robinson for the cover design

Chris Wright

Jeff Kagohara in Brazil

Joan Wright

About the Author

Alan Wright was an award-winning BBC radio and television presenter for over 25 years and today speaks and broadcasts around the world.

His series for young people, Kitten Cuthbert, has really taken off and he frequently speaks to educational conferences and to schools and colleges about making learning fun.

His new novel *Here Today* has been a labour of love and reflects his admiration for the Beatles and their music, as well as their influence on the modern world.

More here –

        www.afterdinnerspeakeralanwright.co.uk

        www.kittencuthbert.com

Also by Alan Wright

*Available worldwide from Amazon
and all good bookstores*

www.mtp.agency

www.facebook.com/mtp.agency

@mtp_agency

www.ingramcontent.com/pod-product-compliance
Lightning Source LLC
LaVergne TN
LVHW041646060526
838200LV00040B/1743